MAGIC
WORDS

HOW TO GET
WHAT YOU WANT
from a NARCISSIST

LINDSEY ELLISON

MAGIC Words: How to Get What You Want from a Narcissist

www.lindseyellison.com

ISBN 13: 978-1-989161-48-7
ISBN 10: 1989161480

Published by
Hasmark Publishing
www.hasmarkpublishing.com

This book is dedicated to my brave clients and readers.
The fictional scenarios written here came from
your stories of heartbreak and frustration. Thank you for
trusting me to guide you. You are my inspiration.

Acknowledgments

When I decided to write an unconventional book on how to communicate with a narcissist, I have to admit, I had my doubts. I doubted whether I would have the time to write it, whether it would sell or fail, whether anyone would read it, or whether it was a good idea at all. So when in doubt, we create a team of people who can love, support, and motivate us, and can offer objective feedback. This is my team, and I cherish all of you.

To my husband, Will, my greatest fan and supporter. Thank you for cheering me on.

To my editor, Laura Oliver – your love of the pen makes you invaluable and insightful, and I couldn't have written this without you. You're a class act, and an inspiration to all writers.

To my coach, Rachel – you have changed the way I view

the world. Without your support, I wouldn't have written this.

To my brother, Michael – thank you for reading my early drafts and providing me with your thoughtful feedback. I'm so lucky to have you as my brother.

To my parents – thank you for believing in me and pushing me to write and keep going. Your support means the world to me.

To my girlfriends, the "Riva Divas." It has taken a lifetime to find girlfriends who are supportive, non-judgmental, and willing to listen. Our long nights of red wine and trying to solve the world's problems helped me write this book. Love you girls.

Table of Contents

1

Introduction

In 2010, after 10 years of marriage, and 17 years of being together, I made the frightening decision to separate from my husband. I was 35 years old with two little boys, who were, at the time, four and seven years old. I didn't know why I had to leave the marriage; I just knew I had to. Throughout our years together, and even from the earliest months of our courtship, I knew something was off, but I could never quite pinpoint it.

On the surface, my husband was doting, nurturing, and attentive, but his love always came with conditions. In return for his affection, I was to behave as he wanted me to, never question his decisions, and subscribe to his belief system. Should I step outside those silent rules and have a boundary, I would pay for it dearly. Yet his "punishment" was always so subtle, covert, and manipulative, that I never recognized it as punishment, much less emotional abuse. He was an expert at stonewalling, gaslighting, and using passive aggression to make his point; so accomplished at this that I always ended up apologizing, not really understanding what I was apologizing for. After an argument, I was often dazed and confused. But apologizing, I discovered, would restore his equanimity, thus granting me temporary peace. Our relationship existed on a fragile foundation, and I silently endured being married to a man who was "perfect" to the outside world but an emotional time bomb behind closed doors.

By the time I was 30 years old, I had begun to question his behavior. It took me five long years with a therapist to understand that his behavior would never change and to find the strength and courage to leave the marriage. Aside from childbirth, it was the hardest thing I've ever done. After telling him I wanted a divorce, I was sucked into his maddening vortex of negotiation, apologies, false promises, sadness, heartbreak, bullying, and threats, sometimes all in one day, sometimes all in one hour.

I did everything I shouldn't have done. I engaged, tried to reason with him or change his mind, cried with him, apologized, responded to his threats in sheer rage, changed my mind to make him feel better, only to change my mind again after he bullied me. The more I tried to establish boundaries, the more his behavior worsened:

1. He acted like the victim of my "irrational" aggression and decision-making
2. He taunted, poked and prodded me so that I would lose my cool (which I always did)
3. After any hysterical outburst, he posed as my rescuer,

subtly implying that I could not survive without him nor would anyone else deal with my hysteria

4. He questioned my mental state and used bipolar disorder as a potential amateur diagnosis

I had no idea how to fight back other than to plan an escape route and break free from him. I moved out of the marital home and rented a place of my own. When the news of our separation broke to my family and social circle, people were shocked, even devastated. When they'd ask me the reason for my "sudden" escape, I couldn't give a solid answer. Without a logical testimony on my part, and his explanation that he was "abandoned" for "no reason," I was shunned by nearly our entire circle of friends.

But my battle was far from over. Our divorce took over two years, and I ended up giving in to many of his requests out of sheer exhaustion. I walked away with zero assets, lost any rights to my marital home, went without child support for two years leaving me nearly broke, and agreed to abandon my rights to his pension and part of his 401K, which were legally owed to me. To this day, I bear the financial setbacks from that crappy deal, but I consider myself lucky. I have talked with too many people who've endured far worse outcomes.

As I slowly emerged out of my hell and put more time and space between my husband and me, I began to realize how dysfunctional our marriage truly was. Grief, for the loss of a life I always wanted, turned to anger. I began to investigate the pathology of our breakdown. It wasn't until a year into my separation that I fell in love with someone new, only to be betrayed and quickly discarded. Heartbroken and depressed,

I hit rock bottom that I didn't think was possible. Back in therapy, but this time with a new therapist, I learned of the term "narcissist."

After that first session, I drove from my therapist's office straight to the bookstore. I stumbled on a book titled *Narcissistic Lovers: How to Cope, Recover and Move On* by Cynthia Zayn and M.S. Kevin Dibble. Standing in the self-help section of Barnes and Noble, I thought, *How did I not know about any of this? If someone told me about narcissism and clued me into my codependency, I would have left a long time ago!*

My anger fueled my thirst for more understanding of this personality disorder. I read book after book, delved into learning about codependency, which helped me understand my childhood, and how the death of my mother when I was six years old left me gravely afraid of abandonment. Every moment of my free time was spent researching, looking for answers, and connecting even more dots. Meanwhile, I documented all that I learned and began writing articles. My early work debuted in *Huffington Post*, and one article went viral, *The #1 Secret on How To Engage With A Narcissist*, which was then translated by Huff Post into four other languages. The viral response to the article not only surprised me, but it indicated how prevalent the problem is and the lack of information underserving its victims. I vowed to change that, and thus, my new career in coaching and writing was born.

A few years into coaching people worldwide, I became aware of another systemic problem for which there were no resources. While some have the blessing of a no-contact relationship with their former abuser, many still have to endure some form of contact due to co-parenting, family ties, professional attachment, or a protracted court battle.

I decided to re-examine how we communicate with narcissists and create a different strategy. I thought about my former career as a marketing and advertising executive, where we would spend months developing a communication strategy on behalf of our clients for their target audience. In the early phases of our development, we would research audience behaviors by conducting focus groups, quantitative and qualitative analyses, learn about their fears and their triggers, and identify "words of influence" to persuade their buying behaviors. From there, we created audience personas, gave the fictitious buyers names, noting where they shopped, what foods they liked, what kind of cars they drove, etc. Finally, the communication plan – exactly what to say and how to say it to the prospective buyer – was executed. Marketing 101.

Our typical communication *modus operandi* in our relationships is born of emotion – fear, love for our children, hate, or frustration. It's about what we want, what we fear, what could happen to our children, etc. The classic mistake is that we engage believing that the narcissist actually cares about us, our needs, or sadly, even our children, whom we share.

This book is about learning how to communicate with the narcissist in your life. After advising so many clients on how to create a persuasive strategy by specifically using language a narcissist will respond to, "MAGIC words," and seeing the profound results it gives them, I realized I needed to share this. Not only has it benefited me personally, but I have passed on this knowledge to my children who employ these words as best they can.

Some things to note and important caveats: these words are NOT foolproof. This book and its MAGIC words are suggestive and not prescriptive. They are also not intended, nor ever considered, to make your narcissist a better person. If you think your narcissist will change, please put this book down and first read other books that will educate you on narcissism and other personality disorders that are a subset of pathological narcissism. This book is for the reader who has been struggling with a narcissist in his or her life for a long time and who already has a substantive understanding of all the behaviors associated with this mind-boggling disorder.

This book is intended to help you look at your narcissist through a different lens and provide a healthier (and hopeful) perspective on your difficult situation. Narcissists are bullies and resort to pathetic, child-like tactics when they don't get their way. Yet it baffles me that despite their juvenile behavior, we are still intimidated by them and feel powerless against them. Remember this: children do not fully understand logic, therefore, neither do narcissists. Instead, they respond to simple, carefully-selected words that make them think they are getting their way.

Create a strategy. Use your words. Stay within the MAGIC.

2

CEO of Your Life

Imagine this: you're the CEO of a major food label, and you have a brand new line of peanut butter you need to sell, and you want me to buy it. Based on your consumer research, you know that I'm a busy working mother, and making fancy lunches isn't always realistic. Your research also indicates that because I'm a working mother, I may be fearful that I'm not doing enough for my children.

So, in order for you to persuade me, you must use words that play on my deepest fear: *If I don't make the best choices for my children, I may not be a good mother.* You then brainstorm a number of words that speak to my fear and you settle on one that would have the most impact: "Choice." By making the best choices, I would, by default, subconsciously feel empowered and confident as a mother. Therefore, your magic word combination is: *"Choosy Moms Choose Jif."*

Boom! I just bought your peanut butter.

Now, notice what you *didn't* do. You didn't tell me that you just manufactured 1 million jars of peanut butter and that if you don't sell them, your investors will be up your ass, putting you in jeopardy of losing money, your job, your house, or your marriage. And when that didn't work, you didn't emotionally plead with me, saying how much it would mean to you if I bought your peanut butter, or that it would hurt you deeply if I didn't. And when that didn't work, you didn't tell me that I'm a horrible person, and how the HELL could I be so stupid for not buying your amazing peanut butter? And when that didn't work, you didn't block me from ever trying to buy your peanut butter again, and should I step into ANY store where you sell peanut butter, you'll sue me! (Does this reaction sound familiar?)

Instead, you created a MAGIC business plan, assessing my personality type and fears, which allowed you to successfully persuade me to buy, which helped you achieve your goal. Now, stay within the CEO mind-set, but shift to a business you do own: *your life.* Your life has many different "products:" your job, kids, wellness, happiness, finances, relationships, etc. So how do you create a "business plan" that persuades a narcissist to support each of these products? You stay focused on your goal, avoid emotion, and use the most effective words repetitively, if necessary.

When dealing with a narcissist, every encounter must be thought of as a business deal. You always have to be two steps ahead of his thinking. You must be proactive, not reactive. You must make a plan and have a strategy.

Here's how to perform MAGIC:

M – Map their persona

A – Assess their fears or insecurities

G – Goal set

I – Identify your words

C – Communicate

In each step, I will offer a template for you to use, and to help you, I'm going to fill in the following template using a fictional narcissist, whom I will call "Bill."

3

M – Map Their Persona

In marketing and advertising, persona development is a critical step for the communication strategy. It often requires months of research before you can map one specific buyer persona, but the good news for you is that you likely have years of research under your belt. Now, all you need to do is document your research and map his persona using the following template.

Bill the Narcissist

1. *Describe Bill's mother and her relationship with him:*

Elaine is a very unhappy person and likely a narcissist herself. She left a promising career because she got pregnant with Bill, and she resents her son because he "stole" her future. She took out her frustrations on him and always pushed him to "be his best." In one way, she didn't want her son to turn out like her, but in another way, she resented him even more for his successes. Bill could never win his mother's appreciation or affection, and even today, he still tries to win her over. They have a very unhealthy relationship, but as much as she resents him, she still sides with him when conflict involves me. The more he hates me, the more she praises him. She has two other sons, and she was always easy on them. Bill, however, is seen by Elaine as an extension of herself, and she continues to interfere.

2. *Describe Bill's father and his relationship with him:*

Jack is a kind yet passive man and doesn't say much to Bill other than boring small talk. Deep down he is ashamed of himself and hates the fact that he allowed his wife to bully his son. He is proud of Bill but unable to express how he feels, and because of that, he feels even more shame. Bill and Jack have a cordial, yet distant relationship, and now that Jack is much older, he has given up trying to make it any better.

3. *What is the relationship between Bill's mother and father?*

Jack and Elaine have been married for 43 years, yet they

should have divorced a long time ago. Elaine rules the roost. When they were younger, they argued often, but Jack finally realized he would never win and now functions on autopilot. Because Elaine never had a career or employees to manage, she treats Jack as if he were her subordinate and constantly berates him for his own career choices. No matter what Jack does, including making plenty of money, it is never good enough.

4. *If Bill has siblings, describe each of them and their relationship with him:*

Bill has two younger brothers, Scott and Trevor. Scott coped with his unhappy parents by being a model student, avoiding conflict, and flying under the radar. He went into the military and is now a high-ranking officer. Bill rarely sees him because Scott has been on multiple deployments. Bill described Scott as being the "lucky one" who got out of the house and chose a career that would prevent him from coming home. Trevor was always a nice kid and a "mama's boy." He had girlfriends and a much easier life than Bill. As a teen, when Trevor brought his friends over, his mother would do anything for them. But when Bill brought his friends over, his mother picked on and embarrassed him. Bill always resented Trevor for being perfect and resents him even more now. Trevor is a wealthy doctor, married to a beautiful wife and has three beautiful daughters. One can hardly mention Trevor's name in front of Bill because he will fly into a fit of rage for no reason.

5. *What do you think Bill needed as a child and didn't get?*

Bill needed to be seen as an individual and for his strengths, not as a shadow of his brothers, a disappointment to his mother, and a shame trigger to his father. He was a smart, sensitive kid with much to offer, but every time he tried to shine, his mother put him down. He still craves his mother's attention and approval, and she gives him just enough to make him hope for more. He also needed a father who could stand up to his wife. Now that Bill is the "strong one" or rather, the "bully," his mother respects him. They have an odd relationship where Bill acts like the husband Elaine always wanted. Bill needed unconditional love, praise, attention, and, most of all, kindness. No one was kind to Bill. He was pitied or punished for not being the person his mother hoped he would be.

6. *Thinking about this marriage, what were the things that brought the two of you together and the things that broke you up? (I will answer as if I'm in the same situation with Bill to illustrate how this works.)*

In the beginning, Bill was so amazing. He was charming, funny, and successful. After we married, everything changed. He was no longer nice or charming. He was irritable, angry, always yelling at me for no reason, and blaming me for things that had nothing to do with me. When I finally had enough and demanded that he change, he got even worse. I asked him to go to marriage counseling, and he refused. The more I tried to help and get closer to him, the more he detached. He stopped coming home on time, or he took long business trips without calling me. I finally discovered he was having an affair. I filed for divorce, and it's been hell ever since.

7. Describe your relationship now:
Horrible. He refuses to cooperate, and co-parenting is a nightmare. No matter how reasonable I try to be, he accuses me of being controlling or overbearing. He is always so angry, and we can never have a pleasant text exchange without him saying something mean, and that triggers me to say something mean back, and then he always ends up winning. I don't understand how he's the one who cheated on me yet, somehow, he is always the victim, and I'm the "aggressor." Our relationship is exhausting and takes a toll on my mental health every day.

8. What are the recurring sources of conflict between you?
I ask him to do something, and because I'm the one asking, he refuses to do it. If I were to ask him to take our child to the Emergency Room so I could be home with the baby, he would likely refuse or call me horrible names before he decided to go to the hospital. And if he did go, he would blame me for the emergency, call me an "unfit mother," and tell me I should thank him for helping me out, despite the fact it was his child who needed him. Conversely, if he asks me to do something, like have the kids for a few hours longer, or switch weekends with him, and I say no, he blows up my phone with vitriolic texts until I finally concede to his demands.

9. *What does he dislike most about you? What does he always tell you?*

He calls me controlling and thinks I'm an overbearing mother or that I worry too much about the kids. Actually, everything he accuses me of is a projection of what he does to me. Everything he hated about his mother, he now hates about me. It's interesting that since our divorce, he and his mother are closer than ever. Oh my gosh, I think I get it! He interprets my behavior as if I'm his controlling mother. No wonder he acts like such a child.

10. *Outside your relationship with Bill, how do others perceive him, and how does he perceive himself?*

Everyone loves Bill. They think he's handsome, charming, brilliant, and an excellent father. Since he has his own business, he doesn't have anyone to report to, which feeds his narcissism even more. Bill justifies his affair by claiming I never gave him the attention he needed, ignoring the fact that I was caring for our two small children. He blamed me for my lack of interest in sex and demanded I stopped breastfeeding because I was ruining my body. And somehow, he is able to tell this version of our history to everyone in his social circle and receive support through this "difficult" time. The more he plays the victim, the more attention he gets.

11. *What is most important to Bill?*

Praise; to win; to possess the best of everything – best house, car, girlfriend, kids, vacations, etc. He lives with the hope that one day his mother will finally adore him like she does her other sons. It is vital to perpetuate his greatness and false sense of self to ruin anyone who threatens his grandiosity.

4

A – Assess Their Fears or Insecurities

Now that you have carefully mapped your narcissist's persona, the next step is to assess his fears or insecurities. You will use what you have written in his persona to gather content for this section. Don't worry if your answers duplicate each other; you will tally your answers in the final part of this step, which I'll explain in a moment. Here's your template:

1. *Looking at your answer in question 1 above, what does Bill fear or feel insecure most about when it comes to his mother? (It's okay to brainstorm here. There is no wrong answer).*
   Never being his best; lack of love and approval; Being a shadow of his brother; Abandonment of his mother's love and attention.

2. *Looking at your answer in question 2 above, what does Bill fear or feel insecure most about when it comes to his father?*
   He's afraid he will be a wimp like his father; that his wife (or any romantic partner) will end up bullying him like his mother did to his father; he is terrified of being ashamed because he knows that is a recipe for being controlled; being shameful means being weak.

3. *Looking at your answer in question 3 above, what does Bill fear or feel insecure about when it comes to his parents' relationship?*
   Being controlled and berated by a woman; not being good enough in the eyes of his wife; settling for less than what he deserves; staying in an unhappy marriage.

4. *Looking at your answer in question 4 above, what does Bill fear or feel insecure about when it comes to his relationship with his siblings?*
   Not being good enough; not having the perfect life like his brother, Trevor; being in the shadow of affection rather than in the spotlight.

5. *Looking at your answer in question 5 above, what does Bill fear or feel insecure about in his childhood?*

Being a shadow; not being seen for his greatness; being overlooked; being perceived as pathetic or weak; still being a disappointment to his mother.

6. *Looking at your answer in question 6 above, what does Bill fear or feel insecure about in your marriage?*
Lack of attention, criticism, apparent weakness, being exposed as a fraud.

7. *Looking at your answer in question 7 above, what does Bill fear about you or feel insecure about in your existing relationship?*
Being controlled, exposed, losing face.

8. *Looking at your answer in question 8 above, what does Bill fear or feel insecure about regarding your recurring sources of conflict with him?*
Being controlled; looking weak, particularly to his kids; being subordinate, not in control.

9. *Looking at your answer in question 9 above, what does Bill fear or feel insecure about you?*
That I'm a better parent; that the kids will like/respect me more; that I will hurt him as his mother did; expose him as a fraud.

10. *Looking at your answer in question 10 above, what does Bill fear or feel insecure about in terms of how others perceive him and how he perceives himself?*
He fears that people will discover the truth about him: that he's a bully, fraud, cheater, and weak; that he's just like his mother, the person he resents the most; that he

isn't good enough; that people won't see him, which puts him at risk for being back in the "shadows;" should anyone expose the truth, his entire "kingdom" could crumble.

11. *Looking at your answer in question 11 above, what does Bill fear or feel insecure about in terms of what is most important to him?*

He fears criticism; losing; that he is average; his mother abandoning him once again; that because he seeks "the best" of everything, and that I represent "the worst" of everything, my very existence threatens his entire fantasy that he is trying so desperately to sustain.

Excellent. Now, your final step is to tally the key words and fears that you described above and, next to each, provide a numerical value as to the number of times they were mentioned, as I do here:

Key words and fears:

Not ever being his best – (2)

Lack of motherly love and approval – (2)

Being a shadow of his brothers – (3)

Abandonment of his mother's love and attention – (2)

Being a wimp or weak; appearing to others that he is weak – (6)

Being controlled (or bullied) like his mother was to him – (8)

Being ashamed – (1)

Not being good enough – (5)

Being like his mother – (2)

Exposure that he is a fraud – (4)

That he will lose and I will win – (2)

That I'm a better parent – (1)

That the kids will like/respect me more than him – (1)

That I will destroy and hurt him, just like his mother did – (1)

Looking at my list, you will see that Bill's top three fears or insecurities are:

1. Being controlled (or bullied)

2. Being a wimp or weak; appearing to others that he is weak

3. Not being good enough

Now that I know the top three, I will use words or phrases that play on, or mitigate triggering, his fears. I will also keep the remaining list handy for when a difficult engagement occurs, and I encounter communication barriers.

But let's assume, for a moment, that this is your list. I'd like you to think about your entire engagement history with your narcissist, and ask yourself whether your communication has always triggered his top three fears. Perhaps you've texted him constant reminders about your children's well-being or given "helpful suggestions" on how to parent. But when he doesn't respond, you, out of frustration, used harsh words that suggested he was a wimp or weak. You may now realize why your approach has never worked.

Rather, if you use words or phrases that give him the perception that he is in control, strong, and making wise decisions, you are more likely to get what you want. Now, I'm sure the thought of implementing this strategy makes you nauseous or resistant. Check in with your ego: If you're thinking, *Why the hell should I be nice? He doesn't deserve to win*; or *it would feel unauthentic or manipulative*, go back to the beginning of this book. How you feel about your narcissist should be irrelevant. This is a business deal, and having feelings or emotions will only get you sucked into what I call the Narcissistic Vortex: the chaotic abyss of hell, with the intent of confusing you enough that you'll back down.

Your list of fears and insecurities is a powerful asset. Think of it as a secret manual that will help you decode confusing and odd behavior and keep you from having an emotional response. It should also empower you. Your entire history with this person has been about *you* fearing *him*. But once you do this exercise, you'll realize that *he's* been fearing *you* all along.

5

G – Goal Set

If you and I were engaged in a business deal, and you wanted me to buy your product, we'd likely set up a meeting to negotiate and agree on the terms. But because you're a smart CEO, you wouldn't just walk into the meeting without a strategy or knowing what your bottom line pricing is. You must do the same for when you engage with your narcissist, and you must do this every single time. Because each engagement is different and may trigger different fears or insecurities, you must first ask yourself: What is your desired outcome?

Let's bring back Bill to illustrate how this might work. Bill and I share custody of our two sons, who are eight and 11 years old. My 11-year-old, Peter, wants to sign up for an after-school drama program, which costs $600. Bill makes twice as much money as I do, but our divorce agreement states that we each have to pay for half the cost of enrichment activities. My desired outcome, therefore, would be for Bill to agree to Peter attending and to get him to pay for half of the program.

Next, I look at my list of fears and insecurities and answer these questions:

1) *How might my desired outcome trigger him?*

Bill's top three fears are: Being controlled (or bullied); being weak; appearing weak; Not being good enough. Being that narcissists see their children as an extension of themselves, Bill is unable to see Peter as an individual with unique desires outside of his grandiose world of perfection. Therefore, Peter attending a drama program might trigger Bill's fear of being perceived as a wimp or weak. And because he fears being controlled (or bullied), he might perceive that I am "forcing" a wimpy activity on my child, despite Peter's desire.

2) *How can I capitalize on his fears or insecurities and then neutralize? (I also look at my longer list of his fears or insecurities to determine where else I might gain leverage.)*

a) Being controlled (or bullied) as his mother did to him
Potential strategy: Communicate that this was Peter's choice; using words to suggest that Bill is making the decision, not me.

b) Being a wimp or weak

Potential strategy: Identify some of the most "manly" actors in Hollywood and say that Peter said he wanted to be like one of them (i.e., Clint Eastwood, George Clooney, etc.)

c) Not being good enough (or not ever being his best)

Potential strategy: Communicate how much Peter has been praised by his teachers for his acting ability and that he has "real talent;" that Peter has been identified as being "the best" by his teachers.

d) That I am a better parent (or kids will like/respect him more)

Potential strategy: that Peter told me should he get into the program, he couldn't wait for his dad to see him on stage; suggest opportunities for how Bill might shine should he agree.

3) *What emotional response will I avoid should he not oblige with my desired outcome, and what will I do instead? (This is for you to be mindful of your own triggers.)*

I will not respond by calling him names or attacking the very fears I'm trying to neutralize. Instead, I will observe his response and offer empathy as a way to subconsciously placate his need for mothering and approval.

4) *What am I willing to give up or "negotiate" to achieve my desired outcome? (Note: When dealing with narcissists, there is an unspoken rule to never negotiate with them. However, in this case, you want to give them the perception that you are negotiating because when they feel like they are winning, they are more likely to concede. Here, you want*

to come up with other things that are important to them or things they want from you, but only pull from this should you really need to.)

He recently asked me for an extra weekend with the kids, which I'm willing to give up should he agree. I would offer driving Peter to and from rehearsals, even on the days that Bill has him. I normally don't like his mother being around me and the kids in the same room, but I know how much he still needs praise from his mother, so I might suggest buying his mother a front row seat ticket on opening night, which would come as a gift from Peter.

Based on my potential responses outlined above, you may be wondering whether Peter did say he wanted to be one of those actors or whether his teachers did praise him for his "talent." Of course, this is a fictional scenario, but let's just say, "kind of." While I don't advise outright fabrication of the truth, merely because it could backfire should the actual truth be revealed, I do advise "stretching the truth," when necessary, to get what you want. By now you've realized that telling the whole truth and nothing but the truth with your narcissist has never worked. The true art of persuasion is being two steps ahead of your decision maker and saying things that will make him feel good.

This entire strategy may make you feel uncomfortable, or perhaps you are appalled that I am even suggesting it. But let me be frank: you are reading this book because you've been doing the same thing over and over, expecting a different result, which is the definition of insanity. Applying logic to the illogical will never work. Being rational with the irrational will never work. Manipulating a manipulator, however, will give you way better results. Now, let's put this whole thing together by giving you the words to make magic happen.

6

I – Identify Your Words

Before you get started, let's discuss the purpose of this section. The following words and phrases are suggestive, not prescriptive, and are in no particular order of preference. They are to help you think differently about how you communicate, and the key word here is think.

———————————

Often when we communicate with narcissists, we hardly think at all before we respond. Instead, we respond out of emotion or frustration. Each time you must engage with your narcissist, go to this section and identify words or phrases that will help you draft your request or response. You can choose from multiple words suggested here or alter them to make them authentic to your voice. Once you get the hang of it, these words will come naturally to you and, hopefully, you will no longer need this book as a reference. As you establish your new way of communicating, you may even come up with new words that aren't even mentioned here. If you do, I'd love to hear what worked for you, so please visit my website at www.lindseyellison.com and send me a note. Who knows? Maybe there will be multiple editions of this book. We are all in this together!

———————————

1   I hear you

A narcissist's top agenda is always to be heard or seen. Think back to what you may know about his childhood. One or both parents were probably narcissists, who could never provide unconditional love and support. Being that narcissistic parents see their children as an extension of themselves, they are unable to see their children as unique individuals. Your narcissist, therefore, received "love" only on the condition that he behaved in accordance with his parents' ideals. He maintained their conditional love by creating a false sense of self: one that would suit his parents' narcissistic vision and one that would gain love and admiration outside his parents' nest. Once he realized this coping mechanism drew in a fan club that compensated for the lack of love and praise, he relied heavily on this supply to sustain his survival.

Being heard is a drug to him – he can never get enough, and should his supply run low, he will do anything to get his next fix. You may have observed that sometimes your narcissist can be nice, and show signs of normalcy, which may even appear as empathetic. And at one point, you likely fell into his trap by letting your guard down, thinking that *maybe* he was starting to change. Don't be fooled – his supply was low, and he was looking to you to fill his ego tank.

So when you see your narcissist displaying child-like behavior such as a temper tantrum, incessant texting, or trying to get his way, try responding with, "I hear you," and then repeat back to him exactly what you heard (or read).

I hear you **Examples:**

I hear you. You are concerned that Peter may get bullied because he chooses drama over playing football. That's a fair point. Let me think about that.

■

I hear you. You are concerned that if I take half of your 401K, I am not deserving of it because I didn't work and chose to stay home with the children. I see how this upsets you. Let me think about that and get back to you.

■

I hear you. You are concerned that if my mother watches the children instead of having them in after-care, you won't have access to them on your days. I can see why this might be perceived as a problem. Let me talk with my mother about your concerns and get back to you.

Notice how these examples don't suggest you agree with his concerns. You're just hearing and observing them. By hearing them, you are giving him the immediate supply he needs, which thereby neutralizes the escalating tension between you. By saying, "I'll get back to you," you maintain control and buy time to respond. Or, you may choose not to respond at all, which leads me to my next suggestion.

2 Say nothing

A narcissist loves a good argument. The more he engages with you, the more opportunities he has to break you down, insult you, and get his way. Of course, when his words are hurtful or blatantly wrong, you likely respond by telling him how wrong he is, hoping that you will change his mind. Once again, you get sucked into the Narcissistic Vortex. Reminder: you will *never* change his mind because he doesn't value anything you say. So stop trying.

When he has made his point, and you've made yours, and no agreement has been reached, stop engaging with him. For instance, after you tried the "I hear you" approach and told him you need to think about it, he might not be satisfied with your response. So, he might go to Defcon 2 and up the ante by name-calling or insulting. This is where you walk away and say nothing.

After you put your text notifications on silent or program your email to automatically put his messages into a special folder, at some point, you will have to reengage with him about something else. And because you don't want to delete his texts or emails in case you need to document his abuse, it is likely you will read his defamatory tirade. This is where I see clients fall off the strength wagon.

When you allow his words to weaken you, you are giving away your power. A narcissist is an emotional vampire. He is never equipped with authentic power so he must steal power from others, and you have been his consistent source of supply.

Until now.

Let's say you have a four-year-old child who asks you for a snack just as you're preparing dinner. You tell your child, "No, we will be eating dinner in about 15 minutes, so you'll have to wait." But your child stomps her feet, throws her crayons on the floor, and demands she eat something now. You continue to say no. Her tantrum escalates and gets more dramatic. She tells you she hates you and you are a horrible mother. Do you give in? Do your feelings get hurt? Do you question your motherhood skills? Hopefully, your answer is no to all the above. Why? Because you know she's a child who doesn't know any better. She has yet to mature and develop appropriate communication skills. You are smarter and more capable than she is. And should you argue or rationalize with her, you get stuck in a power struggle. Instead, you might put her in timeout, redirect her, or ignore her tantrum completely and carry on with dinner preparation.

There is no difference between how you would ignore a four-year-old's temper tantrum and a tantrum of a narcissist. Your narcissist is disabled by a disorder. He is emotionally handicapped. So why on earth would you take anything personally from an adult who acts like a toddler? See how easy this is?

Say nothing **Examples:**

(this is a visual, albeit metaphorical, representation of saying nothing)

Now, once he has calmed down, you can try the strategy suggested on the next page.

If... Then... 3

As discussed earlier, narcissists love a good game, and they love winning. Losing is a result of an enforced boundary, and narcissists despise boundaries. Boundaries are like kryptonite to a narcissist – they weaken him. And being that weakness is something he deeply fears, he will do anything to avoid boundaries. This is why trying to negotiate with a narcissist feels nearly impossible. Healthy people respect boundaries, so you make the natural mistake of assuming your narcissist will respect yours. So when you are trying to get something from him or prevent him from getting something from you, you must make it appear that he is winning no matter the scenario. I know this is incredibly difficult to do, but you can navigate this by pulling ideas from your Goal-setting exercise to form your "If...Then..." MAGIC words. Once again, I will answer as if I'm in the same situation with Bill to illustrate how this works.

1. *What do you want (or what don't you want) from this engagement?*
   I want Bill to agree to have Peter sign up for drama classes and to pay for half of it.

2. *What does he want (or what doesn't he want) from this engagement?*
   He won't want to pay for it and will suggest he do a more "manly" sport.

3. *What does he fear about this engagement?*

That Peter will be viewed as weak by his peers, which would reflect poorly on Bill.

4. *What other fears and insecurities (from your list) might play a role in this engagement?*

The perception that I am controlling; I am a better parent; not being good enough.

5. *Outside of this engagement, what else might he want from you that would make him feel like he's winning? (You can think of former requests that you've denied, or perhaps ignored.)*

Switching weekends; Asking me to reimburse him for Peter's new cell phone.

Great. Now, you can get creative and have some fun with this.

Try this formula:

**If (what you want + the opposite of his fear),
then (his perceived benefit).**

If… Then… **Examples:**

If Peter enrolls in drama, and you are willing to sign him up, then Peter will be so excited – he told me he couldn't wait to act out his lines, and he said he was saving them up just for you.

– *What you want* = enrolls in drama

– *The opposite of his fear (control)* = offering for him to control the process

– *Perceived benefit* = That he is the better parent because Peter is sharing something *only* with Bill.

If Peter enrolls in drama because his teacher thinks he's a superstar, then everyone else will get to see how great he is.

– *What you want* = enrolls in drama

– *The opposite of his fear (being weak)* = teacher thinking he's a superstar

– *Perceived benefit* = If more people get to see how great Peter is, then more people get to see how "great" Bill is.

And if all else fails, you may have to consider giving up something he asked of you, but only if it's not that important to you. But of course, you won't reveal it's not important; you will pretend that it's very valuable.

■

If Peter enrolls in drama, it shows him what a supportive father you are to him (he will so appreciate that), then "I'm willing to give up my weekend that you requested, even though we had plans." (or…) "I can pay for the cost of the drama, and we can call it even on the cell phone reimbursement since it's the same cost."

– *What you want* = enrolls in drama

– *The opposite of his fear (being a fraud)* = Bill is supportive and appreciated

– *Perceived benefit* = He won a weekend and didn't have to pay for the class.

■

Of course, your statements don't have to be as rigid as shown above. You can move things around so that it feels comfortable and natural. Merely use the formula as a guide to help you brainstorm different approaches.

I trust that

4

Narcissists are notorious for being pathological liars. The more they lie, the more they believe their lie as a truth. Lying protects their fraudulent truth, which gives them supply when someone falls for it. In the past, you may have called your narcissist a liar out of frustration or anger. Naturally, this approach didn't work because calling him a liar only threatens his false sense of self. If you want something from him, you must appear to be playing along with his fictional narrative. You may also look at your list of fears and insecurities and find words to neutralize them.

I trust that **Examples:**

I trust that we will co-parent through this.

■

I trust that you'll also see the benefits of Peter taking drama classes.

■

I trust that your agreeing with me on this will show Peter how much you support him.

■

I trust that you'll drop the kids off on time because I know how punctual you like to be. Thank you.

Everything is going to be okay

When narcissists don't feel as if they're in control, they get anxious, panicky, or hyper-focused on the issue at large. You might have once made the false assumption that you both will logically and rationally discuss the issue, only to find yourself back in his vortex. Should a problem or concern arise, take a step back and observe his behavior. If the issue requires mutual problem-solving, the worst thing you can say is, "Don't worry. I'll take care of it." You're just setting him up for another temper tantrum.

See him as a child and use the phrase, "Everything is going to be okay," and then explain why all is under control. This isn't a patronizing voice but one that is truly sincere. Remember, if your narcissist lacked mothering in his childhood, he might subconsciously find reassurance and calm with this approach. Always add in other reassurances that might neutralize his fears or insecurities.

Everything is going to be okay **Examples:**

Everything is going to be okay. I realize you can't attend Peter's doctor's appointment, but I will take notes and text them to you the moment the appointment is finished.

■

Everything is going to be okay. We already agreed to 50/50 custody, so my taking the kids on a trip this weekend only means that you will gain a weekend another time.

■

Everything is going to be okay. Peter can still do a sport on the days he doesn't have drama classes, as we've already enrolled him in karate.

You are so good at

6

I think this one goes without saying why it is effective. Narcissists love praise and affirmation that they are good at everything. But I realize that this one may be the most difficult for you because you know the only thing he is good at is lying and deceiving. You'll only use this phrase when you need something from him. The beauty of this phrase is that it naturally neutralizes the fears and insecurities that all narcissists have: they're not good enough. When you say this, he will be pleased that you're finally noticing how great he is (and hey, what took you so long?).

You are so good at **Examples:**

Could you take Peter to soccer practice? You're so good at coaching him because you were the star athlete at his age, much better than I could ever do.

■

Could you look at this proposed schedule? You're so good at managing your time that I thought you might appreciate looking ahead.

■

Could you help Peter with his math homework? You're so good at math and numbers that you're a much better tutor than I could be.

Which would you like?

When my kids were younger, I became a master at the game, "Which would you like?" If I wanted them to eat their vegetables, I'd ask, "Which would you like? Would you like to go to bed early or eat your vegetables?" Surely, they chose the latter because going to bed early was the less appealing option. But the reason it worked is that they felt empowered to make a choice themselves without my telling them what to do. The same strategy can work for your narcissist because he wants to be in control. When you want him to do something, think of a lesser appealing option that pairs with your request. Of course, you'll want to be a bit savvier with your options than the example I used with my children; otherwise, they will think you are placating them.

Which would you like **Examples:**

Which would you like? For Peter to do drama and karate or nothing at all?

■

Which would you like? Do you want me to drop the kids off late, where you will only see them for one hour instead of three, or would you like to pick them up yourself?

■

Which would you like? You could take my settlement offer now and save money, or you could fight me on this issue and spend thousands more dollars on attorney fees.

The lawyer reminded me that…

8

(or therapist, teacher, mentor, etc.)

If you're no longer under your narcissist's spell, he no longer values you or what you tell him. That's why it can be advantageous if you mention the opinion of a respectable third party to reinforce your position. You may even go as far as suggesting that the third party would commend him should he comply with your request.

The lawyer reminded me that…
Examples:

Your mother reminded me that you were wheat intolerant as a child, so I think it's best if the kids were to avoid it. She'd be impressed if you told her that, as you have a great memory.

■

The pediatrician reminded me that it's normal for kids to gain weight before a growth spurt, so we don't have to worry about Peter. The doctor remembered what a good athlete you are and suggested staying active when you're with him.

■

Your lawyer reminded me that you are willing to comply with the agreement and said that you are willing to do this as smoothly as possible. I appreciate that.

You seem stressed. What can I do to help?

9

(or angry, irritated, distant, etc.)

When a narcissist has a negative emotion, his goal is to transfer that onto you so that you can occupy this emotion and then exhibit aggressive behavior. Should you take the bait, your happy mood turns into anger, and you yell and curse, exactly at the time he turns calm and deviously questions your mental health. This bait and switch, also known as gaslighting, is a narcissist's most dangerous weapon. Don't fall for it.

Instead, when his mood begins to turn, and he accuses you of doing something that he is actually guilty of, calmly call him on it and then ask how you can help him. I have to admit; this is one of my favorite MAGIC words because it stumps them every time. To be clear, you're not really going to help him with his said emotion; you're just deflecting his attempts to bait and switch.

You seem stressed. What can I do to help? **Examples:**

You seem agitated that I'm trying to schedule the kids' activities. What can I do to help?

■

You seem confused by the offer that was presented to you. What can I do to help?

■

You seem stressed that I'm not willing to comply with your schedule change. What can I do to help?

■

His likely response might be with increased negativity, but not to worry. Just ignore it. Simply end the conversation with, "Let's discuss this when you're less agitated. I hope you can work things out."

You might benefit from

10

A narcissist loves to win, but he can't always see the winning element of what you're proposing. So, why not suggest it for him? Even if there isn't an obvious benefit, make one up, and see if he bites. Feel free to get creative, but don't take it too far or, once again, he might sense you are playing him.

You might benefit from **Examples:**

You might benefit from quality time with your child, should you agree to…

■

You might benefit from saving money, should you agree to…

■

You might benefit from a bigger house, should you agree to…

■

Whatever he is benefitting from, try to align it with one of his fears or insecurities so it has greater impact.

7

C – Communicate

Now, it's time to communicate your MAGIC, so how do you get started? First, understand that not every one of these phrases will work for every scenario. This is about trial and error. Over time, you will know what words create MAGIC, and they will be second nature to your vocabulary. Second, feel free to get creative with these. Move words around, or join one suggested word with another suggested phrase. You'll likely come up with new words not even suggested here. If so, please share them with me so I can pass on the MAGIC.

But if you find that none of these words works because your narcissist is pathologically unreasonable, keep using them anyway. The MAGIC formula is designed to help you keep your cool and stay out of the Narcissistic Vortex. It's also meant to show you that he is the problem and for you not to become part of the problem. Ross Rosenberg, author of *The Human Magnet Syndrome: The Codependent Narcissist Trap*, advises us to observe, not absorb. Therefore, look at the problem; don't become it.

Finally, when you first try these words, be prepared for your narcissist to question your motive. He might mock you for trying to be "smart" or patronize you for sounding so vague. Your shift in communication is essentially a boundary. Since a narcissist is threatened by boundaries, he will strike you where it hurts. If he does, don't be discouraged that this approach isn't working because it is. Stay the course.

Once you employ the MAGIC and start seeing the benefits, you may have a startling discovery: you once played a role in the dysfunction by joining him in his game. In order for a narcissist to win, he must always have an opponent in the arena. A narcissist's game is a lot like tennis; he can't win unless someone else is on the court hitting the ball back to him. And for years you've been returning his serves, blindly thinking the game will be even. While some are lucky to leave the match entirely through no-contact, it doesn't mean you're permanently chained inside the arena either. Through MAGIC, you will be able to walk onto the court, serve your ball, and then walk away. No longer will you be the "John McEnroe" and emotionally react to every volley. You'll play your game and then leave. You will win some, and you will lose some. But if you're consistent, over time, your narcissist will find you boring and then find another amateur player to trap in his arena.

Finally, the key to your success is loving yourself. Employing MAGIC words requires strength and confidence, and self-love is the driving force. If you've been with a narcissist for many years, loving yourself may feel odd and uncomfortable, likely because you've been brainwashed into thinking it's wrong. But let me offer a metaphorical analogy that might help you.

Think of yourself as a gas stove (sounds weird, but go with it). When you first met your narcissist, your flame was at its highest level. After all, your shining light is what attracted you to him in the first place. But as your relationship deepened, his devaluation of you weakened your flame. As time went on, your flame diminished until it was completely extinguished. You felt broken, dead inside, and you had no zest for life. You just survived. Now, here you are, trying to navigate your existing relationship with this person, with no flame to guide you. You may wonder if you have any strength left to begin the MAGIC.

But my dear reader, lest you not forget your most invaluable asset: your pilot light. The pilot light never goes off, even when the flame is gone. Your pilot light is your spirit, your kindred soul, and your relationship with your higher power. *No one* can take this from you. In fact, even when you're dead, your spirit still lives on. It's *that* powerful. Your pilot light – your spirit – is omnipotent. And when you are connected with spirit, and believe in yourself, your flame naturally reignites. Once you realize this, you become a fearless warrior. You are unstoppable. You are, most importantly, unbreakable.

You must make a choice: are you going to give away your power to someone who is powerless, or are you going to keep that power within and reignite your shining light? If you choose the latter, commit to a daily practice of connecting with spirit.

As you close this book, choose to release all negative patterns and narratives you've held on to. Starting today, you're no longer the victim. You're the magical *victor*.

Appendix

Use this section as a handy tool to construct your MAGIC plan. For every conflict you have with your narcissist, continue to refer to these pages to construct a request or response. Over time, you will get the hang of it, and you will no longer need this as a crutch. But, sometimes we can all fall off the wagon and go back to our old patterns of communicating. Not to worry! If that happens, forgive yourself, come back to this book, and create new MAGIC.

M – Map their persona:

1. Describe your narcissist's mother and their relationship

2. Describe your narcissist's father and their relationship

3. What is the relationship between his mother and father?

4. If he has siblings, describe each of them, and their relationship with him

5. What do you think he needed as a child and didn't get?

6. Thinking about your marriage (or former relationship), what were the things that brought you together and then broke you up (or that ended your relationship)?

7. Describe your relationship now

8. What are the recurring sources of conflict between you?

9. What does he dislike most about you? What does he always tell you?

10. Outside your relationship with him, how do others perceive him, and how does he perceive himself?

11. What is most important to him?

A – Assess their fears or insecurities:

1. Looking at your answer in question 1 above, what does he fear or feel insecure most about when it comes to his mother? (It's okay to brainstorm here. There is no wrong answer).

2. Looking at your answer in question 2 above, what does he fear or feel insecure most about when it comes to his father?

3. Looking at your answer in question 3 above, what does he fear or feel insecure about when it comes to his parents' relationship?

4. Looking at your answer in question 4 above, what does he fear or feel insecure about when it comes to his relationship with his siblings?

5. Looking at your answer in question 5 above, what does he fear or feel insecure about in his childhood?

6. Looking at your answer in question 6 above, what does he fear or feel insecure about in your marriage (or your former relationship)?

7. Looking at your answer in question 7 above, what does he fear about you or feel insecure about in your existing relationship?

8. Looking at your answer in question 8 above, what does he fear or feel insecure about regarding your recurring sources of conflict with him?

9. Looking at your answer in question 9 above, what does he fear or feel insecure about you?

10. Looking at your answer in question 10 above, what does he fear or feel insecure about regarding how others perceive him and how he perceives himself?

11. Looking at your answer in question 11 above, what does he fear or feel insecure about in terms of what is most important to him?

12. Now, tally the key words and fears that you described above, and next to each, provide a numerical value as

to the number of times they were mentioned. Keep this list close to you, or take a picture of it on your mobile phone so that you have it no matter where you go.

G – Goal Set

1. How might your desired outcome trigger him?

2. How can you capitalize on his fears or insecurities and then neutralize? (Look at your longer list of his fears or insecurities to determine where else you might gain leverage.)

3. What emotional response will you avoid should he not oblige with your desired outcome, and what will you do instead? (This is for you to be mindful of your own triggers.)

4. What are you willing to give up or "negotiate" to achieve your desired outcome? (Note: when dealing with narcissists, there is an unspoken rule to never negotiate with them. However, in this case, you want to give them the perception that you are negotiating because when they feel like they are winning, they are more likely to concede. Here, you want to come up with other things that are important to them, or things they want from you, but only pull from this should you really need to.)

I – Identify Your Words

1. I hear you

2. Say nothing

3. If… then…

   a. What do you want (or what don't you want) from this engagement?

a. What does he want (or what doesn't he want) from this engagement?

b. What does he fear about this engagement?

c. What other fears or insecurities (from your list) might play a role in this engagement?

d. Try this formula:

If (what you want + the opposite of his fear), then (his perceived benefit)

4. I trust that

5. Everything is going to be okay

6. You are so good at

7. Which would you like?

8. The lawyer reminded me that… (or therapist, teacher, mentor, etc.)

9. You seem stressed (or angry, irritated, distant, etc.). What can I do to help?

10. You might benefit from

C – Communicate

As you begin to employ your MAGIC, remember this is about trial and error. As with any experiment, documenting your outcome from each trial will provide you with data on what worked and what didn't, and ultimately inform your next trial. My clients often practice their MAGIC with me via text or email before they communicate with their narcissist–this gives them "sea legs" before navigating open water on their own. You could do the same with a close friend or family member, and role-play potential responses so that you feel comfortable. If you belong to a divorce or codependency support group, perhaps suggest this book as reading material and partner with each other to practice. Once you get the hang of it, you might even find it "fun" because you discover how easy and empowering it is to be two steps ahead of your narcissist. I will admit, there are days when I enjoy seeing how my MAGIC words yield positive results. Sometimes, it feels good to win, unapologetically.

There will be days, however, when you won't win and you will feel discouraged. Don't let your loss derail your efforts entirely. Stay the course. Use this time to check in with yourself and assess how his behavior is trigging your fears or insecurities. The one benefit (and probably the only benefit) of having been with a narcissist is that it teaches you about yourself and opportunities for self-improvement.

While narcissists have the nasty ability to expose our greatest weakness, they can also unmask our greatest power. One thing you will certainly learn by dealing with the narcissist in your relationship or marriage is that you don't want to go down this road again; this insight improves your chances of having healthy and fulfilling relationships in the future. So, instead of coming out of this relationship feeling broken and downhearted, you can embrace entirely new ways of communicating and finally have what you want and deserve in a relationship.

Resources

With altruistic intent, a few years ago I decided to open my private, client-only Facebook group to anyone suffering from narcissistic abuse. My 50-member group turned into thousands in just a few weeks. It was a disastrous move. In the beginning, I was able to monitor the posts and respond to people's questions and comments. But as the group grew and became too large to monitor, the virtual environment went from supportive to destructive.

Online narcissistic abuse support groups, in theory, are a good idea. However, because so many abuse victims do not seek professional help (often because they are fearful or cannot afford it), they use chatrooms as their only lifeline, allowing them to anonymously unleash their anger and frustration. And when the group has thousands of members, the "support" can turn into toxic, negative, and unproductive rants about their "unsolvable" situation. If you're looking for support with actionable ideas, be wary of these groups or, at the very least, do not get sucked into the rabbit hole of virtual pity parties.

I am living proof that I was able to overcome abuse, and I did so without the help of a support group. My personal growth, and my newfound love of life, came mostly from reading the books I recommend here. My success resulted from researching two genres: clinical and spiritual. The clinical research explored all aspects of narcissism and codependency, so I could understand why and how dysfunctional relationships occur. The spiritual research explored the missing link of self-love, why we lose it, and how to get it back. When I combined the two, something magical happened. Not only did my pain go away, I felt happy and at peace. I hope, through your research, you will find a similar path.

Note to reader: This reading list reflects some of my favorite book titles, and does not fully reflect my years of research and continued work (if I gave you that, you'd be exhausted).

Clinical Resources:

1. *The Human Magnet Syndrome: The Codependent Narcissist Trap* – Ross Rosenberg
2. *Codependent No More: How to Stop Controlling Others and Start Caring for Yourself* – Melody Beattie
3. *Narcissists Exposed: 75 Things Narcissists Don't Want You to Know* – Drew Keys
4. *The Wizard of Oz and Other Narcissists* – Eleanor Payson and Cathryn Bond Doyle

5. *Too Good to Leave, Too Bad to Stay: A Step-by-Step Guide to Help You Decide Whether to Stay In or Get Out of Your Relationship* – Mira Kirshenbaum

6. *Boundaries: When to Say Yes, How to Say No, to Take Control of Your Life* – Dr. Henry Cloud and Dr. John Townsend

7. *How to Break Your Addiction to a Person* – Howard M. Halpern, Ph.D.

8. *Will I Ever Be Free of You?: How to Navigate a High-Conflict Divorce from a Narcissist and Heal Your Family* – Dr. Karyl McBride, Ph.D.

Spiritual Resources:

1. *You Can Heal Your Life* – Louise Hay

2. *Conversations with God* – Neale Donald Walsh

3. *Awaken the Inner Shaman* – Jose Luis Stevens

4. *The Vortex* – Esther and Jerry Hicks

5. *The Law of Divine Compensation* – Marianne Williamson

6. *The Four Agreements* – Don Miguel Ruiz

7. *Rising Strong* – Brené Brown

8. *Anatomy of the Spirit* – Caroline Myss

9. *Change Your Thoughts – Change Your Life: Living the Wisdom of the Tao* – Wayne Dyer

About the Author

Lindsey Ellison is an author, a relationship coach and founder of Start Over Coaching, Inc. She specializes in helping people break free from narcissistic abuse, navigate their divorce or break-up, and find happiness and peace.

Originally stemming from her own personal experiences, Lindsey's mission is to inspire you to make those amazing changes in your life to help you start over and find happiness. She takes you from victim to *victor*.

She can be found at LindseyEllison.com or via her best-selling online course, BreakFreeFromYourNarcissist.com.